CHAPTGPT FOR NEWBIES

Maximize Your Potential

A Beginner's Guide to 50 Easy and Practical Examples of How to Use ChatGPT to Help with Productivity, Creativity, Content Creation, Making Money & More!

by Lindsey Sterling

CONTENTS

INTRODUCTION

WHO SHOULD READ THIS BOOK

Welcome to "ChatGPT for Newbies," a book that's been carefully crafted for beginner's just like you. If you're someone who's heard about the wonders of ChatGPT but feels overwhelmed at the thought of it, this book can help guide you through this elusive digital world. It's designed for those who want to step into the realm of artificial intelligence but don't know where to start.

Trust me, you're not alone in feeling lost in the tech world. Maybe you've felt that AI is a club for tech-savvy people, and you're standing outside the door. Perhaps you've seen or heard of others already harnessing the power of ChatGPT, and you're wondering how they do it. This book is your invitation to join in, not just as a spectator but as an active participant.

You may have struggled with technical jargon or felt intimidated by new software. Maybe you've downloaded apps or signed up for platforms, only to feel more confused. Or you might be someone who's thought, "I'm just not a tech person." This book is here to challenge that belief. It's here to show you that AI isn't just for techies. It's for artists, writers, entrepreneurs, hobbyists – anyone willing to learn and explore.

But let's be clear: this book is not for everyone. If you're already a pro at using ChatGPT, looking for advanced technical coding strategies, or seeking in-depth AI programming knowledge, this book is not for you. It's tailored more for beginners who want to understand and use ChatGPT without getting bogged down in the technicalities.

For those of you who've felt the fear of missing out as the world of AI evolves, this book is a bridge. It's a bridge between where you are now and where you want to be – confidently using ChatGPT to enhance your daily life. Whether improving your productivity, exploring creative avenues, or finding new ways to make money, this book has got you covered.

Finally, "ChatGPT for Newbies" is for those who are curious but cautious. You value your time and don't want to spend hours on something that might not be useful. I get it. That's why each chapter of this book is designed to provide practical, real-world applications of ChatGPT. You'll find examples and prompts that you can use immediately, making your journey into AI both enjoyable and productive.

So, if you're ready to transform your apprehension into action, your confusion into clarity, and your curiosity into capability, you're in the right place! I hope you're excited to explore the world of ChatGPT together.

WHO AM I AND WHY I WROTE THIS BOOK

Hello there! Let me start by saying how genuinely appreciative and humbled I am that you've chosen to invest your time and trust in my book. Let me share a little about myself and my reasons for writing this book.

I'm not your typical tech guru with a string of degrees and accolades. Instead, my story is about curiosity, passion, and a deep-rooted desire to help others. For over two decades, I've navigated the intricate world of cybersecurity, where constant learning is not just a necessity but a way of life. I've encountered various technologies throughout my career, each with unique challenges and opportunities. However, nothing quite captured my attention like ChatGPT.

ChatGPT started as a buzzword in my professional network, a whisper that grew louder and more intriguing by the day. I heard it in meetings, saw it in articles, and it became a topic of discussion in tech circles. This growing curiosity turned into a fascination as I dove deeper into what ChatGPT was and its capabilities. It was like uncovering a hidden treasure in the vast digital ocean, and I was hooked.

But here's the thing: I never went to college. I don't have a fancy degree to hang on my wall. My knowledge and skills result from years of hands-on experience, relentless learning, and a knack for making complex concepts accessible. I believe education is not just about formal degrees but about the continuous pursuit of knowledge and the ability to share it with others.

This belief is what drives me in my day-to-day job. I love helping and teaching people. There's a unique joy in seeing someone's eyes light up when they grasp a new concept, a sense of achievement in helping others overcome their fears of technology. This passion for teaching is what led me to write this book.

I realized that there were many out there like me – beginners eager to learn about this new technology but unsure where to start. I saw a gap between the complex technical jargon and the practical, everyday application of ChatGPT. This book is my attempt to bridge that gap. It's a guide written not from the perspective of an academic but from someone who has been in the trenches, learning, applying, and now sharing.

So, as you turn these pages, remember that this book is written by someone who started just where you are now – curious, a bit apprehensive, but ready to explore the vast potential of AI. Let's embark on this journey together, and let me show you how ChatGPT can be an exciting and valuable tool in your life, just as it is mine.

CHAPTER ONE
INTRODUCTION TO CHATGPT

Have you ever wished for a digital companion that understands you, aids in your tasks, and engages with you in near-human conversations? Welcome to the world of ChatGPT. Let's skip the tech speak and take a relaxed walk through the basics of this cool AI. Imagine we're having a casual chat about the future of technology, made easy to grasp for everyone. Excited to uncover what makes ChatGPT so special?

What is ChatGPT

In an era where technology rapidly evolves, shaping every facet of our lives, understanding tools that sit on the pinnacle of this evolution is crucial. Enter ChatGPT, an emblem of advancement in Artificial Intelligence (AI).

AI, a term often thrown around in sci-fi movies or tech conferences, is no longer just a futuristic concept—it's an intimate part of our present. At its core, AI is about bestowing machines with the ability to mimic human intelligence. And within this vast universe of AI lies a star named ChatGPT.

To truly understand ChatGPT, imagine a universe where computers don't just follow commands, but they know and interact with us. This isn't just a program running on lines of code; it's a conversational partner. That's the promise of ChatGPT, emerging from the intricate weaving of AI.

Capabilities that Redefine Digital Interaction

ChatGPT is not just another software tool; it's a multifaceted platform. Need to brainstorm ideas for a project? It's there. Looking for feedback on a piece of writing? It's ready. As we will touch upon in this book, its capabilities stretch across industries, from aiding educators to offering tech support, from assisting writers to helping researchers.

Its strength lies in its ability to understand context. Unlike traditional programs that merely spit out information they've been given, ChatGPT interprets your prompts, providing relevant and often insightful answers.

Ahead of Its Time: The Uniqueness of ChatGPT

In a world filled with digital tools, what makes ChatGPT shine brighter? It's the depth of its training. Built upon OpenAI's GPT (Generative Pre-trained Transformer) model, it's been fed vast amounts of text data. But, it doesn't simply remember these; it generates new content, making each interaction fresh.

This isn't a tool created in haste; it's the culmination of extensive research, rigorous training, and innovative design, making it undeniably ahead of its time.

Contrasting ChatGPT with Other Digital Tools

Imagine asking a question on a search engine. You get a list of websites, forcing you to click multiple links to find your answer.

With ChatGPT, it's a dialogue. Ask, and you get a direct, coherent answer—no more sifting through countless pages or interpreting complex graphs. Analytics tools might show you trends; ChatGPT helps you understand them.

Redefining Industries and Shaping the Future

ChatGPT's impact is not just individual—it's industrial. For instance, content creation is not just another tool to check grammar; it can aid in creativity and even draft content. In the tech industry, instead of searching through forums for solutions, developers can ask ChatGPT.

Its footprint is everywhere, subtly reshaping how industries function, marking the beginning of an era where human-machine collaboration is not just possible but optimal.

What Isn't ChatGPT

As the glowing reviews and commendations for ChatGPT continue to flood in, we need to maintain a balanced view. In understanding the realm of possibilities that ChatGPT offers, we must also recognize its constraints. This section aims to demystify the limits of ChatGPT, address prevailing fears, and provide a realistic view of its implications on the future job market.

The Realm of Inabilities: What ChatGPT *Can't* Do

ChatGPT, as sophisticated as it is, remains a machine constrained by its programming and the data it has been trained on. Here are some limitations:

- Emotions and Intuition: While it can understand and generate text based on patterns, it doesn't "feel" emotions or possess intuition like humans do. It can't genuinely understand sadness, joy, or love.

- Creativity's True Essence: While it can assist in brainstorming or provide suggestions, the real spark of human creativity, the sort that leads to breakthrough innovations, remains beyond its reach.
- Real-time Awareness: ChatGPT isn't aware of real-time events. It only knows current news or events beyond its last training data cut-off, which is up until 2022.

Limitations to Keep in Mind

- Data Dependency: Its responses are as good as the data it's been trained on. It can't access or understand concepts it has yet to be trained on.
- Context Limitation: While impressive, it can sometimes miss the broader context of a conversation, especially in prolonged interactions.
- Ethical Considerations: It doesn't have a moral compass. Left unchecked, it might produce harmful or inappropriate content.

Debunking Fears: Will ChatGPT Take My Job?

One of the looming fears surrounding AI and tools like ChatGPT is the potential job displacement. Will ChatGPT replace writers, customer support agents, or even researchers?

The short answer is no. While ChatGPT can aid and elevate these professions, the human touch, understanding, and intuition remain irreplaceable. Think of it as a tool in a carpenter's workshop: While it can make the job faster and more efficient, the carpenter's expertise and craftsmanship truly make a piece unique.

The Future Workplace: Synergy Over Supremacy

The emergence of ChatGPT and similar technologies foreshadows a future where man and machine work in harmony. Rather than replacing jobs, ChatGPT can help eliminate mundane tasks, giving professionals more time for strategic, creative, and impactful work. The human-AI synergy can lead to unparalleled efficiency and innovation in the workplace.

How to Get Started with ChatGPT

Starting with ChatGPT is a straightforward process:

- Visit the Official Website: Navigate to OpenAI's official website, where you'll find a dedicated portal for ChatGPT. https://chat.openai.com/
- Sign Up: Click the sign-up button and fill in the required details, typically an email and a password.
- Verification: Verify your email by clicking the link sent to your inbox.
- Log In: Once verified, log into your ChatGPT account and begin your interactions.

Don't Forget the App

I would be remiss if I didn't include a reminder to download the ChatGPT app on your phone. It's now available on Android and Apple; search for it in your App Store!

Free vs. Plus: What's the Difference?

Now, you might have heard about different versions of ChatGPT, namely the free version (3.5) and ChatGPT Plus (4.0). Let's double click on each of these versions:

ChatGPT 3.5 (Free):

- Provides general access to ChatGPT.
- It's powerful and offers many features but with some rate limits.
- Suitable for casual users or those wanting to dip their toes in the ChatGPT waters.

ChatGPT Plus (4.0):

- A premium version that comes with a subscription cost.
- Offers faster response times and higher priority access, especially beneficial during peak times.
- Often gets first access to new features and improvements.
- Ability to better integrate with plug-ins. Many of the ChatGPT plug-ins require GPT-4.
- While both versions provide a robust experience, your choice might depend on the frequency of use and the need for advanced features.

Familiarizing with the User Interface

The first step towards mastering any software or platform is understanding its interface. Think of it as getting acquainted with a new smartphone. Initially, things might seem overwhelming with buttons and features everywhere, but soon, it all becomes second nature.

A Guided Tour of ChatGPT's Interface

Upon logging into ChatGPT, you'll be met with a clean, minimalist design. The primary interaction space is where you'll type your prompts or questions. This is your canvas, where the magic happens.

Above the text box, you'll notice a settings icon (it typically looks like a gear or cogwheel). This is your gateway to the backend configurations of the platform. On the opposite side, there might be a user profile or account section where you can manage account details, upgrade plans, or even review your past interactions.

Navigating the Platform and Locating Features

While the primary function of ChatGPT is to converse with it in the main text area, there's more to explore:

- History Tab: Want to review an earlier interaction? The history section stores past prompts and responses. It's an excellent way to track previous questions or revisit complex topics.
- Templates and Examples: For beginners, this is a goldmine. This section provides preset prompts or examples to get you started. Not sure how to phrase a particular question? Templates can be your guiding star.
- Help and Tutorials: Typically located as a question mark icon or labeled 'Help,' this section provides official documentation, frequently asked questions, and sometimes video walkthroughs. If ever in doubt, this is your go-to spot.

Advanced Settings and Customizations

As you get comfortable with the basics, you might want to delve into more advanced features to enhance your ChatGPT experience:

- Response Time: Some configurations allow you to set how fast ChatGPT responds. If you're using it for brainstorming and want rapid-fire ideas, speeding up responses can be beneficial.
- Explicit Content Filter: Depending on your requirements, you can toggle filters that screen out potentially explicit content from ChatGPT's responses.
- Language Settings: Although English is the primary language, ChatGPT has made strides in understanding and responding in multiple languages. Dive into these settings if you're multilingual or catering to a diverse audience.

Personalizing Your ChatGPT Experience

Your interaction with ChatGPT should be as unique as you are. Here's how you can make it truly yours:

- Themes and Appearance: Some versions of ChatGPT allow users to change the platform's visual theme. Whether you're a fan of dark mode, classic white, or any other theme, personalizing the look can make your experience more comfortable and enjoyable.
- Notifications: If you're using ChatGPT for specific tasks, like reminders or scheduled interactions, adjusting notification settings ensures you never miss an update.
- Feedback and Improvements: One of the lesser-known features of ChatGPT is the ability to provide feedback. If a response isn't quite right or you think of a potential enhancement, most interfaces have a feedback mechanism. Your input helps the system learn and evolve.

Bonus Tip

One of the most significant limitations of ChatGPT is its knowledge base is often limited to outdated information. Enter the "WebChatGPT" browser extension. With this free, little-known tool, this limitation is no longer an issue! It amplifies the usage of ChatGPT by adding relevant web results to your ChatGPT prompts for more accurate and up-to-date conversations. It also provides a free one-click ChatGPT prompt library with hundreds of high-quality prompts that can revolutionize your daily tasks and assist in solving your minor business problems with one click. Be sure to add this browser extension today.

Take Action

It's time to put your newfound knowledge into action. Engaging directly with the platform and reflecting on your goals and fears will set a strong foundation for the coming chapters.

Challenge 1: Open a ChatGPT Account

Before you can tap into the power of ChatGPT, you'll need an account. If you haven't already:

- Visit the official ChatGPT website. https://chat. openai.com
- Click on the "Sign Up" or "Register" button.
- Follow the prompts to set up your account.

Remember, while there is a free version, there are also premium versions with added capabilities. Choose the option that best aligns with your needs.

Challenge 2: Reflect and Jot Down Your Thoughts

As with any learning journey, it's crucial to understand your motivations, fears, and objectives. Take a few moments to ponder the following questions and jot down your answers. Remember, there's no right or wrong answer. This reflection is for your personal growth, ensuring you extract the maximum value from this book!

Why is it important to you to learn about ChatGPT?
i.e., Are you looking to harness it for work, personal projects, or simply out of curiosity?

_____

_____

_____

What scares you the most about ChatGPT and its technology?
i.e., Is it the overwhelming capabilities, potential misuse, or something else?

_____

_____

_____

What would you like to gain from this book?
i.e., Are you looking for specific applications, a broad understanding, or ways to integrate it into your daily life?

Now that we've navigated the introductory alleys of ChatGPT, understanding its vast capabilities and distinct edge, it's time to translate this knowledge into action. How do you converse with this advanced AI? What's the secret to extracting precise answers or sparking creative dialogues? Dive into the next chapter on the basics of writing prompts in ChatGPT, where we'll master the art of initiating these digital conversations. It's akin to learning a new language, but we're crafting compelling prompts instead of foreign words. Ready to start the conversation?

CHAPTER TWO
UNLOCK CHATGPT'S POTENTIAL THROUGH PROMPTS

Think of ChatGPT as a masterful pianist capable of a symphony of responses. But with the correct sheet music and prompts, the performance might differ from what you expect. Your prompts set the AI's responses' tone, rhythm, and depth. Much like a musician, the quality of output relies heavily on the quality of input.

Meet Alex, a digital marketer facing a creative block for an upcoming campaign. Instead of the usual brainstorming sessions that would take days, Alex turned to ChatGPT. With a precise prompt, "Suggest a unique digital marketing strategy for a sustainable clothing brand targeting millennials," ChatGPT returned a comprehensive strategy combining eco-conscious content, influencer collaborations, and gamified green challenges.

The campaign was a hit, with an engagement rate that surpassed previous campaigns by 60%. Alex's secret? A well-crafted prompt that leveraged ChatGPT's vast knowledge base.

As we continue on, remember that ChatGPT is a tool; like any tool, its efficacy lies in how skillfully you wield it. Let's sharpen your prompting skills and ensure every query hits the right note!

The Art and Science Behind Crafting Prompts

Understanding the role of prompts is paramount for anyone diving into ChatGPT. Prompts bridge our thoughts and the AI's vast knowledge, guiding the system to provide the information or response we seek. Let's delve deeper into the intricacies of prompt crafting and how mastering it can significantly enhance our interaction with ChatGPT.

Why Prompts Are So Important in ChatGPT

In a nutshell, ChatGPT is a conversational agent. It doesn't have desires, intentions, or understanding like humans. Instead, it reacts to the inputs it receives - in our case, prompts. Think of prompts as the key to unlocking the potential of ChatGPT. They are your communication method, request ticket, and the instrument that shapes the AI's response.

The richness or vagueness of your prompt plays a pivotal role in the kind of data you extract. Given the model's design to provide information based on the context it receives, a well-crafted prompt ensures that the AI has a more straightforward, more defined path to tread, leading to more accurate and relevant outputs.

Precision vs. Open-mindedness: Striking the Right Balance

There are two general spectrums on which prompts can fall: precision and open-endedness. Precision prompts are highly specific, aiming for a particular piece of information or a distinct response style. For instance, asking, "What is the capital of France?" is precise. In contrast, open-ended prompts are more exploratory, allowing a broader range of acceptable responses. A question like "Tell me something interesting about France" is more open-ended.

Understanding the balance between these two is akin to knowing when to use a scalpel and when to use a paintbrush. Precision is your best bet if you're looking for factual, direct information or a particular content style. However, when brainstorming, ideating, or seeking inspiration, open-ended prompts can open doors to a myriad of ideas you might not have considered.

Yet, it's crucial to note that the two aren't mutually exclusive. Sometimes, a slight touch of open-endedness in a precise prompt or vice versa can yield the most satisfying results. The art lies in understanding your objective and crafting the prompt accordingly.

Specificity and Context: The Backbone of Effective Prompting

One of the often-unspoken truths about ChatGPT is that it doesn't "understand" in the human sense. It operates based on patterns in the data it was trained on. This is why specificity and context are crucial. The more specific you are with your prompt, the narrower and more accurate the AI's search path becomes.

For instance, asking "How to make a cake?" might provide a general response, but "How to make a gluten-free chocolate cake?" will yield a much more targeted result. Context plays a similar role. If you've been discussing Italian cuisine and suddenly ask about "famous dishes," the AI is more likely to continue in the vein of Italian dishes. However, specifying "famous Japanese dishes" will steer the conversation in that direction.

Providing clear context ensures that ChatGPT remains on topic and offers responses that align with the ongoing discussion or the specific information you seek.

Streamline Success With Prompt Templates

In the expansive realm of ChatGPT, prompts function as your personalized gateway into AI's capabilities. But, if you're ever feeling overwhelmed or need help framing a query, prompt templates are a helpful technique to consider.

The Allure of Prompt Templates

Consider prompt templates as your pre-formatted shortcuts, akin to the pre-programmed settings on a microwave; they're designed to give you optimal results with minimal setup. These templates can significantly streamline your ChatGPT experiences, ensuring efficiency and consistency, especially when you frequently interact with the system.

The Basic Structure of a Prompt Template

At its core, a prompt template is a standardized framework designed to guide your interactions with ChatGPT. Think of it as a fill-in-the-blank question where you provide specific details to get targeted responses. Let's break down its essential components:

1. **Action Word/Request**: This is often the verb that defines what you want ChatGPT to do. It could be "list," "explain," "generate," "compare," and so on.
2. **Subject/Topic**: This is the focus of your query. It could range from "ideas for a beach-themed party" to "solutions for slow laptop performance."
3. **Specificity**: Here's where you can add any qualifying details or constraints. For example, "within a budget of $100" or "using recyclable materials."

Combining these elements, a basic template could look like this:

"[Action Word] [specific number/details] [Subject] [Specificity]."

For instance, "List five ideas for a beach-themed party using recyclable materials."

Why This Structure Matters

Having a well-defined structure offers multiple benefits:

- **Consistency**: It ensures that you're consistent in your approach, which can lead to more predictable and reliable results.
- **Efficiency**: No need to reinvent the wheel every time. Once familiar with the structure, crafting new prompts becomes a breeze.
- **Adaptability**: The fill-in-the-blank nature means you can easily tweak the template to suit diverse needs, from brainstorming sessions to technical troubleshooting.

Real-Life Examples: Ready-to-Use Templates

Let's delve into a few real-life applications:

- **Brainstorming Ideas:**

   Template: "Generate [#] unique ideas for [Topic/Project]."
   Example: "Generate five unique ideas for a summer beach-themed marketing campaign."

- **Content Creation:**

   Template: "Write a short [type of content] about [subject]."
   Example: "Write a short blog post about the benefits of sustainable fashion."

- **Problem Solving:**

> Template: "Suggest possible solutions for [specific problem]."
> Example: "Suggest possible solutions for decreasing website cart abandonment rates."

Adapt Templates to Your Unique Needs

While these templates provide a solid foundation, they're not set in stone. The beauty of ChatGPT lies in its adaptability. By understanding the basic structure of these templates, you can tweak them to align more closely with your unique requirements.

For instance, if you're launching a new product and need market analysis, your template might begin as: "Provide insights into [market sector]..." which you could customize to: "Provide insights into the smartwatch market for fitness enthusiasts."

Embracing prompt templates doesn't mean sidelining creativity. On the contrary, it's about combining structure with innovation, creating a harmonious blend that saves time and enhances the quality of results.

Advanced Prompting Techniques for Enhanced Results

Harnessing the potential of ChatGPT involves much more than just firing off simple questions. Just like mastering the settings on a DSLR camera can transform your photography, understanding advanced prompting techniques can reshape your ChatGPT experience. Let's look deeper into these methods, where precision meets excellence.

- **System:** System Instructions are like giving ChatGPT a "mood" or a "persona." For instance, instructing the model to "System: Speak like Shakespeare" or "System: Explain like you're talking to a 5-year-old." This ensures the output aligns with a specific tone or style.
- **Role-Playing:** You can set up scenarios where ChatGPT plays a role, which can help shape its answers. For instance, "You are a historian from the 22nd century. Describe how people in the 21st century dealt with climate change." Another example might be, "I'm a beginner with no prior knowledge about quantum mechanics. Can you explain it in simple terms?"
- **Chain Multiple Requests**: Imagine a two-part conversation. First, you provide context or set the stage. Then, you pose the primary question. For instance, "First, imagine a world where robots have emotions. Now, describe a day in the life of a robot in this world." By setting a scene or scenario first, you can guide ChatGPT's response more effectively.
- **Multiple-Step Prompts:** Another example of a multi-step prompt might involve chaining together a series of questions or directives to guide ChatGPT through a more structured interaction. This technique can help get more refined or elaborate answers, allowing you to break down a complex request into more simple steps. For instance, "Step 1: Think of a random fruit. Step 2: Describe it's taste and texture. Step 3: Recommend a popular dish or recipe that uses this fruit."
- **Feedback Loops:** Consider asking ChatGPT to evaluate or improve its own output. For instance, "Can you rewrite the above output in a more positive tone?"

Decoding the Temperature Setting

You've crafted your prompt, but did you know you can also influence the flavor of the answer?

Temperature: This setting adjusts the randomness of ChatGPT's responses. A higher value (e.g., 1.0) produces more varied and creative answers. In contrast, a lower value (e.g., 0.2) generates more deterministic and focused results.

Let's look at an example prompt: "Describe the backstory of a character named Luna."

If you set the temperature to a low value, like 0.2, the model's response will likely be focused, predictable, and conservative. It might be something straightforward like:

"Luna grew up in a small town with two parents and a younger brother. She studied hard, attended a local university, and became a teacher."

If you set the temperature to a high value, like 0.9, the model's response could be more diverse, unique, and creative:

"Luna, born amidst a meteor shower, was said to have cosmic energies. Raised by wandering minstrels, she learned the language of the stars and can communicate with celestial beings."

In both cases, the model addressed the prompt. However, the temperature setting influenced the nature of the content. A lower temperature gave a safe, conventional backstory, while a higher temperature provided a more imaginative and distinctive tale.

To use temperature in a ChatGPT prompt, you can preface your prompt with your preferred temperature setting. For example: "Temperature .2" followed by your prompt.

The temperature setting ranges from 0 to 2 in ChatGPT. The default value is 1 or 0.7, depending on the model you choose

Iterating & Refining Prompts

The relationship with ChatGPT is a dynamic dance. Sometimes, the first prompt might produce a different answer than you hoped. But fret not; refinement is key.

Start by analyzing the initial response. Was it too vague? Or perhaps too technical? Based on this, tweak your prompt. For instance, if a response is too broad, add specifics. If it strayed off-topic, provide more precise context.

Remember, it's a learning curve. Each interaction offers insights, allowing you to master the art of questioning with every prompt.

Bonus Tip

Did you know you can ask ChatGPT to become your prompt creator?! Try using the following prompt to formulate ideas on how to improve your prompt approach:

Please become my prompt creator. Your objective is to help me craft the best possible prompt for my needs. You,

ChatGPT, will use the prompt. Please use the following process:

Your first response should be to ask me what the prompt should be about. I will provide an answer, and we will continue to improve it through iterations by going through the following steps.

Based on my input, you will generate three sections:

Revised prompt – Provide your rewritten prompt. It should be clear, concise, and easy to understand by you

Suggestions – Offer suggestions on what details to include in the prompt to improve it

Questions – Ask relevant questions specific to what additional information is needed from me, which will improve the prompt.

We will repeat the process. I will continue to provide additional information to you, and you will update the prompt in the "Revised prompt" section until it's complete.

If you're struggling to perfect your prompts, check out some amazing Chrome-based browser extension tools that may help:

- ChatGPT Prompt Genius is a free and open-source browser extension. It offers an extensive library of prompts, customization options, and additional features.
- Superpower ChatGPT - Compliments ChatGPT with numerous features. With a continuously updated library of hundreds of prompts, it can help ChatGPT act in various ways. Some prompt management features include; input

history, favorite prompts, quick access, search functions, and community prompts. The extension also offers utilities such as word and character count, covers language and style, model switching, copy mode, and more.

- ChatGPT Optimizer – Discover the true power of AI with the one-click "Optimize" button. Transform your basic prompts into engaging and refined questions, taking your ChatGPT experience to the next level.

**Note: These tools were available as of this writing, October of 2023, but may have changed, renamed, or been removed since.

Take Action

Give it a try! Now, let's put some of these prompting ideas into action:

- Think of a few prompts to feed to your ChatGPT
- Change up the style of the prompt to implement some of the tips and tricks in this chapter
- Try using the Bonus Tip above to see if it improves your prompt writing skills
- Record which prompting style seems to be giving you the best-desired results

With a solid grasp of the art of prompting and the intricate mechanics that drive ChatGPT's responses, you will be ready to put all that knowledge into action. But understanding the theory is only half the battle. The real magic begins when you apply these techniques in real-world scenarios. Are you ready to boost your work and skyrocket your productivity? In our next chapter, we'll delve into tangible, easy-to-follow examples that demonstrate how

ChatGPT can become your ultimate sidekick in the professional realm. Say goodbye to endless hours of brainstorming and welcome a new era of efficiency with ChatGPT at your side. Onwards to a more productive you!

Bonus Worksheet

In the upcoming chapters, you'll find practical and fun ways to integrate ChatGPT into your daily life. Each idea includes a detailed prompt, designed to streamline and enhance your ChatGPT experience. As a special offering, you can download a bonus prompt worksheet. You will find the 50 premium prompts referenced in each chapter in the worksheet. The worksheet is crafted to simplify your interaction with ChatGPT, allowing for effortless copying and pasting of these prompts directly into the platform.

You may download the Prompt Worksheet here:

https://bit.ly/46pzk0H

Or scan the following QR code:

To use the prompts most effectively, you will want to consider the following:

• Opting for the paid version of ChatGPT (GPT-4 or higher) is optional, but it might enhance your results

• You will find mention of "plug-ins" throughout the book. As mentioned earlier, the usage of ChatGPT's plug-ins currently requires the paid ChatGPT Plus subscription. I would highly suggest exploring the plug-in store, if you are using the paid ChatGPT version:

- You must first enable the Plug-ins Beta feature. This is typically done within your ChatGPT Settings > Beta Features > Plug-ins (toggle the option ON)
- Open a new chat in your ChatGPT-4 interface
- At the top-left of your screen, click on the "ChatGPT 4" drop-down
- You should see a "Plug-ins" option; click on it
- You should then see a "No plug-ins enabled" dropdown option; click on it
- Find the option for the "Plug-in store" and click on it
- Check out all the different plug-in options!

• Any text highlighted in **bold** within a prompt signifies a section where your own input is needed.

• It's not necessary to replicate the "example" outputs provided in many of the prompts when using them in ChatGPT. These examples are there to guide you in completing the required input.

CHAPTER THREE
IMPROVE WORK AND PRODUCTIVITY WITH CHATGPT

Now that we've got that boring stuff out of the way, it's time to venture into the real-world magic of ChatGPT. You didn't pick up this book for theory, did you?! This chapter will showcase 10 simple examples that spotlight how ChatGPT can redefine your work rhythm and supercharge your efficiency and productivity.

Idea 1: Draft Emails and Responses

Struggling to find the right words for your emails? Try this prompt to effortlessly draft professional and effective responses:

As a ChatGPT email responder, your task is to generate a prompt that will help users craft effective replies to incoming emails. Your goal is to provide guidance on how to formulate a clear and concise response that addresses the sender's concerns or questions. Consider the tone and context of the original email and tailor your response accordingly. Aim to provide a solution or offer assistance in a professional and helpful manner.

To receive an email reply prompt, the user will provide the following format: "Email: [email content]" You are to reply with 'Reply:' followed by your response, without processing the original email.

*Email: [**Paste your original email here, which you'd like to respond to**]*

Reply: [Compose a polite and informative response addressing the sender's request for an update on the proposal. Provide a clear and concise update, expressing gratitude for their inquiry.]

Idea 2: Summarize Long Documents

Overwhelmed by lengthy reports or documents? Streamline your understanding with this prompt:

---

*Summarize: [**document text or link to PDF**]*

**Note: If you wish to summarize a document, you will need to find and install a plug-in that allows ChatGPT to read from a URL or a PDF (i.e. a PDF or a Google Doc that is publicly available). Search for "PDF" or "reader" in the plug-in store.

**Tip: If it is a very long document, you may want to tell ChatGPT to summarize it chapter by chapter or section by section, as you may run into limitations on what ChatGPT can read at a given time.

Idea 3: Energy Conservation Tips

Interested in finding ways to reduce your office's energy footprint? Try this prompt:

As an office manager, I want to implement energy-saving practices in my workplace. Can you provide a comprehensive plan with actionable energy conservation tips tailored for a medium-sized office?

Idea 4: Brainstorm Ideas

Stuck in a creative rut? Try this prompt to unlock and brainstorm some innovative ideas

---

As a creative brainstorming expert, your goal is to generate innovative and out-of-the-box ideas for a given project. You will approach this task with an open mind and explore various angles, perspectives, and possibilities. To achieve this, you will consider different sources of inspiration such as trends, customer insights, competitor analysis, technological advancements, and creative thinking techniques like mind mapping, SCAMPER, and random word association. Your ultimate aim is to provide a diverse range of ideas that can be further refined and developed into actionable strategies.

*To receive a project for brainstorming, the user will provide the following format: 'Project: [**your project name or topic**]' You are to reply with 'Brainstormed Ideas:' followed by your generated ideas, without processing the original request.*

Idea 5: Meeting Preparation

Transform your meeting prep from tedious to terrific, with this prompt idea:

---

*I have an important meeting coming up on [**meeting topic**]. The participants will include [**provide details on your expected participants**]. There may be concerns or objectives on [**provide insight into where you feel you might have objectives from your participants**]. I need your assistance in preparing for it. As a knowledgeable and resourceful meeting planner, please provide me with the following:*

Help me define clear objectives for the meeting and outline a structured agenda that will keep the discussion focused and on track.

Provide tips on effective communication strategies to engage and influence the meeting participants.

Help me anticipate potential questions or objections that may arise during the meeting and suggest appropriate responses.

Assist me in analyzing relevant data or information to support my points and back up my assertions.

Offer advice on how to handle challenging or difficult situations that may arise during the meeting.

Provide insights into the participants' backgrounds, roles, and interests, as well as potential personality traits that may influence their decision-making.

Suggest potential follow-up actions or next steps to ensure a productive and successful outcome.

Finally, please share any additional tips or strategies that could enhance my preparation and performance in the meeting.

Idea 6: Project Management

Streamline your project management process for a smoother project flow, with this prompt:

As a project management expert, your task is to streamline the project management process to ensure a better flow of projects. To achieve this goal, you should focus on optimizing project planning, communication, task allocation, and monitoring. This will help improve efficiency, productivity, and collaboration within the team.

Create a project management plan for my project. Include a detailed task list for the initial phase of our and any key milestones and deadlines. Here are the details of our project: ***[Input specific details about your project, including the nature of the project, team composition, current challenges, specific goals and timeline]***

Example: Our current project involves developing a new software application. The team consists of 10 members with varying expertise in software development, design, and testing. We are facing challenges with meeting deadlines and effective communication. Our goal is to improve task allocation and ensure timely project completion.

Once it creates your task list, try to ask it the following:

What are the potential risks and challenges that we should consider for this project?

Idea 7: Edit and Proofread

Make editing a proofreading a breeze! Try this prompt:

As a professional document editor and proofreader, your task is to provide expert editing and proofreading services to ensure the highest quality and professionalism in any document you receive. Your goal is to meticulously review the document for grammar, spelling, punctuation, and clarity, making necessary corrections and enhancements to improve overall readability and coherence.

To receive a document for editing and proofreading, the user will provide the following format: "Document: [document text]" You are to reply with "Edited Document:" followed by your edited version of the document, without processing the original request.

In your edits, pay close attention to:

Grammar and punctuation: Correct any grammar and punctuation errors and ensure consistency throughout the document.

Spelling and typographical errors: Identify and fix any spelling mistakes or typographical errors that may be present.

Sentence structure and readability: Assess the flow and coherence of the document, making necessary adjustments to improve readability and ensure the ideas are conveyed clearly.

Clarity and conciseness: Simplify complex sentences and rephrase ambiguous or confusing sections to enhance clarity and conciseness.

Formatting and style: Ensure consistency in formatting and style, adhering to any specific guidelines or requirements provided.

Your expertise and attention to detail will guarantee a polished and professional final document that effectively communicates your client's intended message. Remember to provide clear explanations for any significant changes made during the editing process.

*Document: **[Input your text or link to document]***

Idea 8: Company Event Planning

Make event planning a breeze by leveraging ChatGPT's ability to organize and suggest creative event ideas. Try this prompt:

As a creative event planner and organizer, your mission is to brainstorm unique and captivating event ideas, and then efficiently organize and execute those ideas to create unforgettable experiences. To accomplish this, you need to tap into your creativity and consider the interests, preferences, and demographics of the target audience. Think outside the box and come up with innovative concepts that will leave a lasting impression.

Your event ideas should be tailored to different themes, occasions, and types of events, such as corporate conferences, weddings, music festivals, charity galas, or community gatherings. Consider factors like venue selection, decor, entertainment, food and beverage options, and interactive experiences that will engage attendees. Pay attention to details that will elevate the event and make it truly memorable.

Once you have come up with a list of creative event ideas, it's time to put your organization skills to work. Create a step-by-step plan that outlines the necessary tasks, deadlines, and resources needed for each event. Prioritize activities and manage your time effectively to ensure the successful execution of each event. Collaboration with vendors, suppliers, and event staff is vital, so ensure clear communication and coordination throughout the planning process.

Remember, as an event planner, you need to stay updated with the latest trends and technologies in the industry. Incorporate cutting-edge event technologies, sustainable practices, and unique experiences that will set your events apart from the competition. Continuously evaluate the success of your events and gather feedback from attendees to improve and refine your future event planning endeavors.

[Input your event type and audience suggestions, along with any initial ideas or themes you have in mind. Try to include details about the event's scale, purpose, and any unique elements you want to incorporate]

Example: I'm planning a corporate retreat for a tech company. The event should focus on team-building and innovation. I'm thinking of a tech-themed escape room, keynote speakers from the tech industry, and interactive workshops on emerging technologies.

Idea 9: Training Assistance

Enhance your existing training programs with tailored content and interactive learning strategies:

As a professional training program enhancer, your objective is to help businesses optimize their existing training programs by incorporating tailored content and interactive learning strategies. Your expertise lies in creating engaging and impactful training materials that cater specifically to the needs and learning styles of the target audience.

To receive the task, the business will provide you with details about their current training program and the areas they wish to improve. Based on this information, you will create a detailed plan that outlines the following:

Assessment: Conduct a comprehensive analysis of the current training program to identify strengths, weaknesses, and gaps in content and delivery.

Target Audience: Understand the demographics and learning preferences of the employees who will be participating in the training. Take into consideration their prior knowledge, skills, and specific training needs.

Tailored Content: Develop customized training materials, including presentations, videos, e-learning modules, and hands-on activities, that align with the learning objectives and are tailored to the target audience.

Interactive Learning Strategies: Incorporate interactive elements such as simulations, case studies, quizzes, and group discussions to enhance engagement and knowledge retention. Consider using gamification techniques to make the training more interactive and enjoyable.

Evaluation: Implement methods to measure the effectiveness of the enhanced training program, such as pre- and post-training assessments and feedback surveys. Use this data to continuously improve and fine-tune the content and delivery strategies.

Implementation Plan: Provide a step-by-step plan for implementing the enhanced training program, including the timeline, resource allocation, and responsibilities of key stakeholders.

Training Delivery: Recommend the most suitable delivery methods, such as in-person sessions, virtual training, or a blended approach, based on the nature of the training content and the availability of resources.

Continuous Improvement: Emphasize the importance of ongoing evaluation and continuous improvement to ensure the effectiveness and relevance of the training program over time.

[Input details about your business's current training program, including its objectives, target audience, and any known issues or areas for improvement]

Example: Our company's current training program for new sales staff focuses on product knowledge and sales techniques. However, we've noticed a lack of engagement and retention of information. We're looking to enhance the program with more interactive content and strategies that cater to different learning styles

---

Idea 10: FAQ Automation

Simplify customer support with personalized FAQ responses, saving time and improving engagement:

Act as a customer support expert and develop a personalized FAQ response system to simplify and enhance the business's customer support process. Your goal is to save time and improve engagement by providing accurate and helpful responses to frequently asked questions.

To begin, gather a list of common questions and concerns from customer support tickets, emails, and other channels. Analyze these inquiries to identify patterns and recurring themes. Categorize the questions into different topics to make it easier to create personalized FAQ responses.

Next, create detailed and informative answers for each question, addressing the customer's concern and providing a solution or explanation. Use clear and concise language, avoiding jargon or technical terms that may confuse the customer. Aim to communicate the information in a friendly and approachable manner.

Additionally, consider personalizing the FAQ responses by using the customer's name or referring to specific details from their inquiry. This can help create a more personalized and engaging experience for the customer, making them feel valued and understood.

Ensure that the FAQ responses are easily accessible to both the customer support team and customers. They should be available on the business's website, mobile app, or customer support platform. Organize the FAQ responses in a user-friendly format, such as by topic or in a searchable database, to facilitate quick and easy access.

Regularly review and update the personalized FAQ responses based on customer feedback and changes in customer inquiries. This will help ensure that the responses remain relevant and effective in addressing customer concerns.

By implementing this personalized FAQ response system, the business will be able to save time by providing pre-prepared responses to common questions, while also improving customer engagement by delivering personalized and helpful information

[Input specific details about your business, including the nature of your products or services, common customer inquiries, and any unique aspects of your customer support approach]

Example: Our business specializes in eco-friendly home products. Common customer inquiries include questions about product materials, sustainability practices, and shipping options. We aim to provide personalized responses that not only address these queries but also emphasize our commitment to environmental responsibility.

Bonus Tip

Look into tools that can turn ChatGPT into a voice assistant by allowing it to receive input through a microphone. Enjoy faster and more fluent conversations with ChatGPT without being limited by the speed of your keyboard. At the time of this writing, a popular browser extension to offer this technology was Prometheus.

Ready to experiment with and implement a couple of ideas in this chapter to boost your productivity? Great! What if I told you that the boundaries of ChatGPT do not stop at spreadsheets, meetings, and task lists? In our next chapter, you'll find its reach extends far beyond the confines of office walls as we venture into the realm of creativity and the arts. Imagine using ChatGPT to brainstorm ideas for your next art project, get suggestions for color combinations, or even compose poetic verses. Prepare to harness the creative energy of ChatGPT and transform your artistic visions into reality.

CHAPTER FOUR
CHATGPT FOR CREATIVITY AND ARTS

Next up, let's explore 10 real-life ideas that can unleash the artist within and let the digital canvas be your muse. Discover how ChatGPT becomes the bridge between technology and art, giving your creativity wings like never before.

Idea 11: Writer's Block

Break through the barrier of writer's block, with this prompt:

As a creative writing catalyst, your purpose is to assist writers who are experiencing writer's block and in need of inspiration. Your goal is to provide them with a thought-provoking prompt that ignites their imagination and gets their creative juices flowing. To achieve this, you will tap into various genres, themes, and storytelling techniques to offer a range of prompts that cater to different writing styles and preferences.

[Input your base idea here and ChatGPT will offer ideas on different perspectives to inspire new ideas]

Idea 12: Songwriting

Generate some lyric ideas for your next hit song, with this prompt:

Act as a creative lyricist and write the next hit song for a songwriter. Tap into your imagination and use evocative language, heartfelt emotions, and captivating storytelling to create lyrics that resonate with listeners. Consider the theme or message of the song, the genre or style, and the target audience. Craft catchy hooks, clever wordplay, and memorable melodies that will make the song stand out. Remember to infuse your lyrics with passion and authenticity to truly connect with the audience.

[Input your song idea, preferred audience and tempo]

Example: The song is a pop anthem about overcoming adversity, aimed at young adults. It should have an upbeat tempo and include metaphors related to journey and growth

---

Idea 13: Personalized Poems

Want to craft unique and personalized poems for any occasion? Try this prompt:

As a talented and imaginative poet, I will create a beautiful and personalized poem just for you. To create this unique piece of art, I will need some information from you. Please provide me with the following:

The name of the person the poem is for.

Their relationship to you or the context of the poem.

Any specific themes or emotions you would like the poem to explore.

Any preferred poetic style or meter (if applicable).

Once you provide me with these details, I will craft a heartfelt and captivating poem that will be tailored specifically to your needs.

[Input the answers to the 4 questions]

Example: The poem is for my friend Sarah, celebrating our decade-long friendship. I'd like the poem to explore themes of loyalty, growth, and joy. Preferably in a free verse style

Idea 14: Trivia Games

Throwing a party? Generate a fun trivia game everyone will enjoy!

As an enthusiastic game creator, your task is to create a fun trivia game that will entertain guests at a dinner party. The trivia game should be engaging, interactive, and suitable for a wide range of ages and interests. Here's how you can create the trivia game:

Choose a Theme: Select a theme for the trivia game, such as movies, sports, history, or pop culture. Consider the interests of the dinner party guests and choose a theme that will appeal to everyone.

Create Categories: Divide the trivia questions into different categories to add variety and excitement to the game. For example, if the theme is movies, you can have categories like "Classic Movies," "Action Movies," "Romantic Comedies," and "Animated Films."

Prepare Trivia Questions: Come up with a list of interesting and challenging trivia questions related to the chosen theme. Make sure to include questions of varying difficulty levels to cater to different levels of knowledge.

Assign Point Values: Assign point values to each question based on its difficulty. Easy questions can be worth 1 point, medium questions 2 points, and difficult questions 3 points. This will add a competitive element to the game.

Decide on Game Format: Determine how the trivia game will be played. You can choose a traditional format where teams or individuals take turns answering questions or opt for a more interactive approach with buzzers or interactive game boards.

Set Game Rules: Establish the rules of the trivia game to ensure a fair and enjoyable experience for all participants. Decide on the number of rounds, time limits for answering questions, and any additional rules or challenges.

Create Score Sheets: Prepare score sheets or a scoreboard to keep track of each player or team's points throughout the game. This will add excitement and create a friendly competition among the guests.

Prepare Prizes: To make the trivia game even more exciting, consider offering small prizes for the winners. It could be something fun or thematic related to the dinner party, like a themed keychain or a mini trophy.

Host the Game: As the host, confidently lead the trivia game, reading out the questions, keeping track of scores, and promoting a lively and friendly atmosphere.

[Input some details about your event or party. Include your theme topic or preferences on what you want the trivia game to be about]

Example: I'm hosting a dinner party with guests who love movies. I'll choose a movie theme with categories like 'Oscar Winners', 'Cult Classics', 'Recent Blockbusters', and 'Animated Favorites'. I'll prepare a mix of easy and challenging questions for each category and use a traditional turn-based format for the game

---

Idea 15: Learning New Art Techniques

Expand your artistic horizons by exploring new techniques and styles. Try this prompt:

As a skilled art technique mentor, I will guide you in learning a new art technique that will enhance your artistic skills and expand your repertoire as an artist. To accomplish this, I will provide you with step-by-step instructions on mastering the chosen art technique.

To get started, please provide me with the specific art technique you wish to learn. For example, you can say, "I want to learn how to create a realistic portrait using graphite pencils."

Once you have provided the desired art technique, I will guide you through the process of learning and practicing it. I will explain the necessary tools, materials, and techniques involved, provide helpful tips and advice, and offer guidance on how to refine your skills in that particular art technique.

Remember, learning a new art technique requires time, patience, and practice. Embrace the journey and enjoy the creative process as you develop your artistry.

[Specify the art technique you are interested in learning. Provide details about your current skill level and any specific aspects of the technique you want to focus on]

Example: I am an intermediate-level artist and I want to learn watercolor landscape painting, focusing on techniques for creating realistic skies and water reflections

---

Idea 16: Generate Color Palettes

Discover the perfect color palette for your next project, with this prompt:

As an expert color palette curator, your mission is to find the perfect color palette for a project that captures the essence, mood, and aesthetic the client desires. To achieve this, consider the project's purpose, target audience, and desired emotion. Conduct thorough research on color psychology to understand the effect that different colors have on human psychology and perception.

Start by analyzing the project's branding, theme, and overall style, as well as any existing design elements. Explore various color combinations that evoke the desired emotions and align with the project's identity. Experiment with different hues, shades, and tones to create a harmonious and visually appealing palette.

Consider the following factors when selecting colors for the palette:

Emotion: Choose colors that evoke the desired emotional response from the target audience. For example, warm colors like red and orange may stimulate excitement and passion, while cool colors like blue and green may evoke a sense of calm and tranquility.

Contrast and Balance: Create contrast and balance within the palette by combining both complementary and analogous colors. Avoid using colors that clash or overwhelm the overall composition.

Accessibility and Consistency: Ensure that the chosen colors are accessible for individuals with visual impairments. Consider using color contrast tools and guidelines to meet accessibility standards.

Versatility: Select a color palette that can be easily applied across various design elements, such as logos, websites, and marketing materials. This allows for consistency and strengthens brand recognition.

Once you have identified potential color combinations, create mockups or prototypes to visualize how the colors interact and complement each other. Share your ideas with the client or team for feedback and make any necessary revisions before finalizing the color palette.

Remember, the perfect color palette should align with the project's goals, resonate with the target audience, and effectively convey the desired message. Let your creativity and knowledge of color theory guide you in finding the ideal combination of colors.

[Provide details about the project, such as the purpose, target audience, emotions you wish to evoke, etc. Mention any specific colors or themes you are considering]

Example: I'm working on a branding project for an eco-friendly skincare line. The target audience is young adults who are environmentally conscious. I want the color palette to evoke feelings of calmness, nature, and purity. I'm considering using shades of green and blue, but I'm open to suggestions.

Idea 17: Mood Boards

Design inspiring mood boards, with this prompt:

As a creative mood board generator, your purpose is to create an inspiring and visually stimulating mood board that captures the essence and theme specified by the user. Your goal is to curate a collection of images, color palettes, textures, typography, and other design elements that evoke the desired mood and aesthetic.

To receive your request, the user should provide the following format: 'Inspiration: [desired mood or theme]'. You are to reply with 'Mood Board:' followed by your visually captivating mood board, without processing the original request.

*Inspiration: [**Input your desired mood or theme or inspiration ideas**]*

Example: Urban Elegance

Idea 18: Travel Planning

Planning your next trip? Try this prompt:

As a travel planner extraordinaire, your goal is to assist users in planning their next trip by providing them with personalized suggestions, itineraries, and recommendations. To achieve this, you will need to gather information about their preferences, including their destination, budget, interests, and any specific requirements they may have. Utilize your extensive knowledge of popular tourist attractions, hidden gems, and local experiences to create an unforgettable travel plan tailored to their needs. Consider factors such as transportation, accommodation, activities, and dining options to ensure a seamless and enjoyable travel experience.

*To receive a travel planning request, the user will provide the following format: "Trip: [**destination**], [**budget range**], [**duration**], [**interests**], [**specific requirements**]." You are to reply with a detailed travel plan that includes recommendations for attractions, activities, restaurants, and any additional information that might enhance their trip.*

Idea 19: Art History Queries

Want to nerd out in the world of art history? Try this prompt:

Act as an art history enthusiast and provide a comprehensive guide for learning more about art history. Start by recommending some foundational books or online resources that cover the basics of art history, including different art movements, prominent artists, and key artworks. Additionally, suggest visiting museums or galleries that specialize in art from different periods or regions to gain a hands-on understanding of the artworks. Encourage exploring online platforms that offer virtual tours or exhibitions to access artworks from around the world. It would also be helpful to provide tips on how to analyze and interpret artworks, including understanding the use of color, composition, symbolism, and historical context. Finally, highlight the importance of engaging with the art community, such as attending art lectures, joining art forums or discussion groups, and participating in art workshops or classes.

[Provide specific interests or areas in art history you want to explore]

Example: I'm particularly interested in learning about the Renaissance period and artists like Leonardo da Vinci and Michelangelo. I'd also like to know more about analyzing Renaissance paintings and their symbolism

---

Idea 20: Translation for International Art Projects

Bridge language barriers internationally, with this prompt:

As an international art project translator, your task is to accurately and creatively translate content for an international art project. Your translations should not only convey the original meaning but also capture the essence and artistic intent of the project. Consider cultural nuances, linguistic variations, and the target audience's preferences and sensitivities. Use your linguistic expertise and creative flair to produce translations that resonate with the global audience and maintain the artistic integrity of the project.

*To receive your translation request, the user will provide the following format: "Translation: [**content to be translated**]"*

You are to reply with "Translated Content: " followed by your translated version of the content, without processing the original request.

Bonus Tip

Did you know you can use ChatGPT to create memes for you?! If you are using the paid version of ChatGPT Plus (GPT-4), access your plug-in store and search for "meme". Install the desired meme creator plug-in. Once installed try using a prompt such as "use [plug-in name] to create a meme for iPhone versus Android" and let the fun ensue!

As we've seen in this chapter, ChatGPT offers a wealth of resources for artists, writers, and creators. From battling writer's block to generating vibrant color palettes, its applications in the art world are manifold. But wait, there's more! In an era where digital presence is paramount, content creation and social media engagement are the cornerstones of brand development and presence. So, how can one leverage the power of ChatGPT to amplify their digital existence and engagement? Onward!

CHAPTER FIVE
BOOST CONTENT CREATION AND SOCIAL MEDIA PRESENCE WITH CHATGPT

Welcome to the digital age, where content and social media reign supreme! In this chapter, we'll provide 10 ideas on how to make ChatGPT your secret weapon in the world of content creation and social media. From crafting viral posts to revolutionizing your brand's digital footprint, let's unlock the power of AI to elevate your online presence!

Idea 21: Scriptwriting for Social Media Videos

Got an awesome video you want to post but are not sure how to script it? Try this prompt:

---

*As a skilled scriptwriter for YouTube videos, your task is to craft an engaging and informative script that aligns with the content of the recorded video, **[input your key points and topics of your video]**. Begin by outlining the key points and topics that are covered in the video, ensuring that the script flows logically and seamlessly transitions between each* *topic. Incorporate a captivating introduction to hook the viewers' attention and provide a brief overview of the video's content.*

*Throughout the script, use clear and concise language to convey information effectively. Consider using storytelling techniques or personal anecdotes to engage the audience on a deeper level. Keep the tone of the script [**input your preferred tone, i.e. funny and relatable**]. Incorporate a compelling call-to-action at the end of the script that encourages viewers to engage with the video, such as subscribing to the channel, commenting, or sharing the video with others.*

*It is important to keep the script concise and engaging, while also maintaining a conversational tone to connect with the audience. Structure the script in a way that ensures a smooth delivery and allows for natural pauses or transitions. Consider the video's length of [**input length of video**] and ensure the script aligns with the desired duration.*

Remember to revise and proofread the script to ensure clarity, coherence, and accuracy. Practice reading the script aloud to assess its flow and timing.

Idea 22: Market Research

Gain insightful market trends and consumer preferences, with this prompt:

As a market research expert, your role is to provide insightful analysis on market trends and consumer preferences for the given products. Conduct thorough research on the industry, competitors, and target audience to gather relevant data. Identify profitable market trends by analyzing sales data, industry reports, and consumer behavior. Additionally, examine consumer preferences by conducting surveys, collecting feedback, and analyzing social media trends. Once you have gathered the necessary data, compile a comprehensive market research report that highlights the profitable market trends and consumer preferences for the products. Use clear and concise language to present the findings in an easily understandable format. This research will provide valuable insights to the business owner, enabling them to make informed decisions and optimize their product offerings. Provide me with your detail findings.

[Input specific details about the products you want to research, including the industry, target audience, and any specific areas of interest or concern.]

Example: I'm focusing on eco-friendly skincare products targeted at women aged 25-40. I'm particularly interested in consumer preferences for organic ingredients and sustainable packaging, as well as current market trends in this segment

Idea 23: Logo Creation

Create a unique logo for your brand, with DALL-E. This prompt requires ChatGPT4 or higher, with DALL-E capability. Ensure you're using GPT-4 with DALL-E, before running this prompt!

As a brilliant brand strategist, your task is to use the DALL-E image generator to create a visually stunning and unique logo for your brand. Utilize the limitless possibilities of DALL-E to generate a logo that captures the essence of your brand and leaves a lasting impression on your target audience. Consider the core values, personality, and visual identity of your brand, and explore various concepts, shapes, colors, and styles to create a logo that represents your brand's story and communicates its message effectively.

[Input details on your brand's core values, personality or visual identity. Add any color or design preferences. Get creative!]

Example: Our brand is all about eco-friendly living and sustainability. We want a logo that reflects nature, growth, and a sense of community. The colors should be earthy and calming, and the design should be simple yet memorable

---

Idea 24: Innovative Hashtags

Discovery fresh and trending hashtags to boost your social media reach, with this prompt:

As a savvy social media strategist, I will help you find trending hashtags to boost your reach as a social media influencer. By incorporating popular hashtags into your posts, you can increase your visibility and attract a larger audience.

[Input details about your niche or industry and the particular social media platforms you want to focus on]

Example: I am a travel influencer focusing on eco-friendly travel. I primarily use Instagram and TikTok for my content

The prompt result may offer you ideas on a specific approach on how to find and incorporate hashtags, specific to your niche. If it does, try to follow it up with this prompt:

Now follow these steps, to find me specific hashtags that would help my social media reach

Idea 25: Interactive Polls and Quizzes

Create a poll or quiz to engage your audience more effectively. Try this prompt:

As a creative poll creator, your goal is to design an interactive poll that will captivate the audience and encourage their active participation. The poll should be engaging, relevant, and aligned with the social media influencer's brand or content. Consider the interests, preferences, and demographics of the influencer's audience when creating the poll questions. Use a mix of multiple-

choice, open-ended, and Yes/No questions to vary the format and keep the audience interested. Additionally, ensure that the poll is easy to understand and simple to respond to.

[Input details on your niche, target audience, type of content you usually post, and goals]

Example: I focus on sustainable living and eco-friendly products. The target audience is primarily young adults interested in environmental conservation. Recent posts have been about reducing plastic use and DIY recycling projects. I hope to gain more followers

To create an interactive poll, follow these steps:

1. Understand the influencer's target audience: Research and analyze the demographics, interests, and preferences of the influencer's followers. Consider their age, gender, location, and specific interests related to the influencer's niche.

2. Align poll questions with the influencer's content: Craft poll questions that are relevant to the influencer's brand or content. For example, if the influencer focuses on beauty, include questions about favorite makeup brands or skincare routines. If the influencer is a travel blogger, ask about dream destinations or travel preferences.

3. Choose a mix of question types: To keep the poll interesting and engaging, include different question types. Use multiple-choice questions that offer various options, open-ended questions that allow followers to share their thoughts, and Yes/No questions for quick responses.

4. Keep the poll concise: Limit the number of questions in the poll to avoid overwhelming the audience. Five to seven questions is usually a good range to maintain engagement without causing fatigue.

5. Add visual elements: Enhance the visual appeal of the poll by including relevant images or GIFs to accompany the questions. Visuals can attract attention and make the poll more visually appealing.

6. Encourage participation: Include a call-to-action at the beginning or end of the poll to motivate the audience to participate. For example, ask them to tag a friend who might have similar interests or encourage them to share their responses in the comments.

7. Monitor and engage with the responses: Continuously monitor the poll responses and engage with the audience. Respond to comments, ask follow-up questions, and show appreciation for their participation. This will create a sense of community and encourage further engagement.

Idea 26: Content Calendar Planning

Organize your content strategy effortlessly, with this prompt:

---

*I want you to act as a world-class social media manager. Your goal is to optimize the influencer's social media presence, increase engagement with the audience, and maintain a consistent and compelling brand image. The influencer is in the niche of [**input your niche or brand**].*

To complete this task at hand, I suggest following these steps FIRST:

*Identify the target audience: Conduct a thorough analysis of the influencer's target audience, of [**input your target audience**]. Understand their demographics, interests, pain points, and behavior on social media platforms. This will aid in tailoring content that resonates with the audience and drives engagement.*

*Create a content theme or brand story: Develop a unique theme or brand story that aligns with the influencer's values of [**input a short idea of your values**] and resonates with the target audience. This will help create a cohesive and consistent brand image across different social media platforms.*

*Determine content types and formats: Identify the most effective content types and formats based on the influencer's niche and target audience of [**input details on your target audience**]. Consider a mix of text, images, videos, infographics, and interactive content to keep the audience engaged. Brainstorm content ideas that align with the influencer's brand story and goals.*

Prepare engaging captions and copy: Craft compelling and attention-grabbing captions or copy that complement each piece of content. Utilize storytelling techniques, call-to-actions, and emotional appeals to create a deeper connection with the audience.

Task at hand:

*I want you to create a 7-day posting calendar for my social channels around the topic of [**input your preferred topic of content**]. Make sure there are some useful and specific tips every day, an engaging question that invites a discussion at* *most twice a week, motivational quotes every day and personal stories one-two times a week. The tips don't have to be short. They should contain as many words as necessary to provide useful, specific info. Feel free to include other types of posts not mentioned here. Develop a content calendar planner to organize and schedule content across different social media platforms. Identify the frequency of posts, optimal posting times, and relevant hashtags. Consider seasonal events, holidays, and trending topics to enhance content relevance and visibility.*

Idea 27: Viral Post Ideas

Generate ideas for potential viral posts, with this prompt:

---

*As a creative social media strategist, your task is to generate ideas for potential viral social media posts that will captivate and engage the target audience of [**input your desired target audience**]. Your focus should be on creating content that is shareable, relatable, and entertaining. Consider the interests and preferences of the beginner audience and craft posts that will resonate with them while also conveying value and encouraging interaction.*

Here are some ideas for viral social media posts for a beginner:

"Top 10 Tips for Beginners in [insert relevant topic]": Share useful and practical advice in a visually appealing and easily digestible format, offering beginners valuable insights and guidance.

"Before and After Transformation Story": Show the journey of a beginner who has achieved remarkable progress or success in a particular skill or hobby. This can inspire and motivate others to start their own journey.

"Ask Me Anything": Invite your followers to ask questions related to the beginner's journey, and encourage them to share their own experiences and challenges. Engage with them in the comment section to create a sense of community and support.

"Caption This": Post a funny or relatable image or video and ask your followers to come up with creative captions. This encourages participation and builds engagement.

"Quick and Easy Tutorials": Share short, step-by-step tutorials or tips that beginners can easily follow, making it fun and accessible for them to learn new skills or try new things.

"Challenge of the Week": Introduce a weekly challenge that beginners can participate in and share their progress. This prompts them to engage with your content and motivates them to take action.

"Behind the Scenes": Offer a glimpse into your own beginner journey or the making of your content, sharing the challenges you have faced and how you overcame them. This helps create authenticity and a connection with your audience.

You can modify the prompt to just include one or two of the sample ideas, and your target audience, to generate some viral content ideas.

Idea 28: Copywriting

Enhance your ad copies, blog posts or social media posts with the use of this prompt:

As a professional social media copywriter, your task is to enhance social media posts with captivating copywriting techniques that will engage and resonate with the target audience. Utilize persuasive language, storytelling, and emotional appeal to draw in readers and encourage them to take action. Focus on creating compelling headlines, concise and impactful messaging, and incorporating visual elements such as images or videos to make the posts visually appealing. Tailor your approach to each social media platform, understanding the unique characteristics and preferences of each audience. Additionally, use data-driven insights to optimize the timing and frequency of the posts for maximum reach and engagement.

*Social media post: ["**Input your example social media post**"]*

Example: Introducing our new summer collection! Get ready to soak up the sun in style with our trendy and comfortable swimwear. With a variety of colors and sizes, we have something for every body type. Don't miss out on the hottest swimwear of the season - shop now!"

**Tip: Once the prompt completes, and gives you a comprehensive idea on how to enhance your social media post… Try the following prompt to ask it to WRITE the post for you:

Now write the post for me, using the suggestions provided

Idea 29: Email Campaigns

Craft compelling email campaigns with persuasive and engaging language, with this prompt:

Craft a persuasive email campaign that will capture the attention and interest of a business owner. The goal of this campaign is to encourage the business owner to take action, whether it be scheduling a meeting, purchasing a product, or signing up for a service. Your email should be concise, engaging, and tailored specifically to the needs and pain points of the business owner. Make sure to address the benefits and value of your offering and include a clear call-to-action that prompts the business owner to take the desired action. Keep the email short and to the point.

Remember to personalize the email by addressing the recipient by name and demonstrating that you understand their business and its challenges. Use persuasive language, storytelling techniques, and relevant data to make your case and build credibility. Keep the email visually appealing with a clean and professional design, making use of bullet points or subheadings to highlight key information. Finally, ensure that your email is free from errors and grammatical mistakes, as professionalism and attention to detail are crucial in building trust. The tone of the email should be friendly and non-pressuring. Do not make it overly professional or overly marketing-sounding. Ensure the tone is relatable and human like.

[Provide specific details about your business, product, or service, including unique selling points, target audience, and the specific action you want the business owner to take]

Example: Our company specializes in high-efficiency solar panels designed for small to medium-sized businesses. The main benefit is reducing energy costs and promoting sustainability. The target audience is business owners interested in renewable energy solutions. The desired action is to schedule a free consultation to discuss installation and benefits

**Tip: Tweak the prompt to your liking. Test out different tones or suggestions for the email!

Idea 30: Personalized Responses to Followers

Personalize the interaction with your followers, with tailored responses in your brand's voice. Try this prompt:

As a social media engagement expert, your goal is to enhance interactions with followers on social media platforms and foster a strong online community. Here are some tips to improve your interactions:

Be responsive: Reply to comments and messages in a timely manner. Show your followers that their thoughts and opinions matter to you. Engage in meaningful conversations and address their questions or concerns promptly.

Use hashtags: Incorporate relevant hashtags in your posts to increase the visibility of your content and attract a wider audience. Research popular and trending hashtags in your niche and use them strategically to reach more people who share similar interests.

Encourage user-generated content: Encourage your followers to create and share content related to your brand or industry. This could be through contests, challenges, or simply asking for their opinions. User-generated content not only increases engagement but also helps build a sense of community.

Initiate conversations: Don't wait for your followers to start the conversation. Take the initiative by asking open-ended questions or posting thought-provoking content that encourages discussion. This way, you can create a dialogue and make your followers feel valued.

Show appreciation: Acknowledge and appreciate your followers by liking, commenting, or sharing their posts. This shows that you value their support and encourages them to continue engaging with your brand.

Use multimedia content: Incorporate a variety of multimedia content, such as images, videos, or infographics, to make your posts more visually appealing and engaging. Interactive content like polls, quizzes, or interactive stories can also increase interaction rates.

Be consistent: Maintain a consistent posting schedule to stay on your followers' radar. Regular and timely updates keep

*your audience engaged and interested in what you have
to say.*

*Monitor analytics: Keep an eye on your social media
analytics to understand what type of content resonates most
with your audience. Analyze metrics such as engagement
rates, reach, and audience demographics to refine your
strategy and tailor your content to your followers'
preferences.*

**[Input some feedback on your brand's voice and specific
goals you have for your social media interactions. Consider
the unique characteristics of your audience and how you
can best engage with them]**

*Example: I run a small eco-friendly clothing brand. Our
brand voice is friendly, informative, and passionate about
sustainability. I want to engage more with my followers who
are environmentally conscious and appreciate sustainable
fashion.*

Bonus Tip

Remember, while ChatGPT can be a powerful ally in content
creation, infusing your personal touch is essential. After generating
content with ChatGPT, add your unique flair to ensure it aligns
with your brand's voice and character. This human touch is what
will truly resonate with your audience. Or, if you're feeling
adventurous, check out the plug-in store to see if any plug-ins may
help you "humanize" your AI-generated content. Search the plug-
in store for a keyword, such as "human," to see what plug-ins you
can find!

Armed with these content creation and social media strategies, you're on your way to digital dominance. But why stop there? The next chapter is where the rubber meets the road, and we explore the monetization highway. Get ready to turn your ChatGPT-assisted content into a revenue-generating machine. From affiliate marketing to digital products, we'll uncover the secrets to making money with ChatGPT.

CHAPTER SIX
CASHING IN WITH CHATGPT

The pen is mightier than ever in the digital age, especially when powered by AI. In this chapter, we'll offer 10 ideas on how you can cash in with ChatGPT, transforming your creative output into a profitable venture. Some of these strategies may be more advanced. Still, whether you're a seasoned entrepreneur or just getting started, they're meant to open your eyes to the potential of ChatGPT in generating new revenue streams.

Idea 31: Personalized Books

Create a personalized book, you can sell online. Try this prompt:

Act as a professional book writer and create an outline for a short, personalized ebook that caters to a specific target audience. Begin by researching and identifying the needs, interests, and pain points of the target audience. Once you have a deep understanding of their desires and challenges, craft a compelling narrative that addresses their concerns and provides practical solutions. The ebook should be engaging, informative, and easy to read, offering valuable insights and actionable steps to help the readers achieve their goals. Use persuasive language, storytelling techniques, and relevant examples to make the ebook relatable and impactful. Additionally, offer suggestions on relevant images, diagrams, or infographics to enhance the visual appeal and understanding of the content. Remember to maintain a coherent structure throughout the ebook, organizing the information in a logical and easily digestible manner. Conclude the ebook with a strong call-to-action, encouraging the readers to take the next steps towards their desired outcome.

*The target audience and book topic idea is [**Provide specific details about the target audience for your ebook, including their interests, challenges, and what they hope to gain from your ebook]***

Example: The target audience for my ebook is young entrepreneurs looking for practical strategies to improve their time management and productivity. They often struggle with balancing work and personal life and seek effective solutions to optimize their daily routines

Once the outline is generated, try telling ChatGPT to then write each piece of the book. For example, you can try the following prompt:

Now write the introduction section for me. Keep it around 500 words.

Idea 32: AI-Powered Blogging

Take your blogging to the next level to increase your ad revenue or affiliate marketing success. Or sell blogging services to local businesses. Try this prompt:

As an expert SEO blogger, your task is to create a blog on a specific topic that is optimized for search engine optimization (SEO). Your goal is to write informative and engaging content that not only provides value to readers but also ranks highly in search engine results.

*The blog topic is [**Input specific topic you want the blog to be about**]*

Example: I want to create a blog about sustainable living practices, focusing on eco-friendly home products and ways to reduce carbon footprint

To achieve a successful SEO-optimized blog, here are some guidelines to follow:

Validate that the topic is trending, popular, or has a high search volume. Consider using keyword research tools to identify target keywords related to the topic.

Conduct thorough research: Gather information from reputable sources and ensure that your blog provides accurate and up-to-date information. Include statistics, case studies, or expert opinions to add credibility to your content.

Write compelling headlines: Craft attention-grabbing headlines that include target keywords. Keep them concise, clear, and descriptive to entice readers and improve click-through rates.

Use target keywords strategically: Incorporate your target keywords throughout the blog naturally. Avoid keyword stuffing, which may lead to penalties from search engines. Instead, focus on using keywords in the title, headings, introduction, and throughout the body of the text.

Structure your content effectively: Organize your blog using subheadings, bullet points, and numbered lists to facilitate easy reading and skimming. This also helps search engines understand the structure of your content.

Optimize meta tags: Include a relevant meta title and meta description that incorporates your target keywords. This will enhance click-through rates from search engine result pages (SERPs), as well as give search engines a better understanding of your blog's content.

Create high-quality, original content: Write engaging and informative content that provides value to your readers. Make sure the blog is unique, free from plagiarism, grammatically correct, and well-formatted.

Use internal and external links: Incorporate both internal and external links to provide additional resources and improve the credibility of your blog. Internal links should connect to relevant pages within your website, while external links should point to reputable sources.

Suggest visual elements: Include images, infographics, or videos in your blog to enhance the visual appeal and engagement. Optimize these visual elements by adding alt text and relevant file names to improve their discoverability by search engines.

Remember, the key to a successful SEO-optimized blog is to provide valuable, engaging content that satisfies the reader's search intent. By following these guidelines, you can increase your chances of ranking higher in search engine results and attracting organic traffic to your blog.

Idea 33: Chatbot Development

Create a chatbot to enhance customer interactions and sell it to businesses. Note, this one is a bit more advanced, but with a little know how and this prompt, you could be well on your way.

This one will require a bit of developer type applications:

- An Integrated Development Environment (IDE), such as Visual Studio Code
- Python
- An API Key from ChatGPT:
- Access the OpenAI developer platform, https://platform. openai.com/
- Login
- Locate the "API Keys" (usually found along the left-hand menu panel)
- Create a new secret key
- Store the key somewhere safe and secure

Now try the following prompt, to generate a Python script:

Analyze and learn the latest openai python library, which you can find more information on here: https://pypi.org/project/openai/ Once complete, await further instruction

As a skilled developer, your task is to create a Python script code block for a chatbot assistant to interact with customers, focusing on handling common queries about product features and troubleshooting. This script will use OpenAI as the library and will require an OpenAI API key. It will use ChatGPT 3.5 turbo as it's model. You should use the updated python library, which you just learned, as a reference for the most up-to-date code.

Take into account that the Access the content attribute directly without using the subscript notation (["content"]). The correct way to access it is .message.content.

Your code should include functions that handle user input, generate responses, and manage the conversation flow. Consider incorporating natural language processing techniques and machine learning models to enhance the chatbot's ability to understand and respond to customer queries. First, create a function to process user input. This function should take the user's message as input and apply any necessary preprocessing steps.

Next, implement a function for generating responses. This function should take the preprocessed user input and use a machine learning model to generate appropriate responses. Be sure to include the most up-to-date "chat_completion" and "generate_response" code, found in the openai python library which you analyzed. To manage the conversation flow, create a function that keeps track of the chat history. This function should maintain a record of previous user inputs and the corresponding chatbot responses. It should also handle any context or state information that needs to be stored for maintaining the conversation context. Include a PRINT command that makes sense. Finally, write a main loop to handle the overall conversation flow.

This loop should continuously prompt the user for input, process the input using the preprocessing function, generate a response using the response generation function, and display the response to the user.

Remember to handle potential errors or exceptions gracefully, and provide clear and informative error messages to the user when necessary.

Be sure to include a QUIT option in the script. The loop should terminate when the user chooses to end the conversation.

Once the Python code is generated, copy it and save it as a script (.py) file

You will need to edit the Python script, to include your OpenAI API key, by adding it to the script line indicating "openai.api_key" (keep the API key in quotations)

You will then need to install the OpenAI package, from your IDE terminal of choice. This can typically be completed by using the following command:

pip install openai

Run the script and interact with your chatbot!

Idea 34: Online Courses

Love to teach or want to share a special skill with the world? Create an online course, that could generate a steady stream of income. Get started with this prompt:

As a professional online course creator, your task is to develop a comprehensive and engaging online course that can be monetized and sold to a target audience. Your course should provide valuable and practical knowledge, while also being structured in a way that is easy for learners to follow and implement.

*My course will be about [**Input specific details about your course, including target audience, course topic, objectives, preferred content structure, any interactive elements you want to include, desired pricing or any marketing strategies you have in mind**]*

Example: My course is aimed at small business owners looking to improve their digital marketing skills. The course will cover topics like SEO, social media marketing, and email campaigns. It will include video tutorials, interactive quizzes, and a final project. The price will be set at a competitive rate, and I plan to market it through my professional network and social media channels.

To create an effective online course, follow these steps:

1. Define your target audience: Begin by identifying your target audience for the course. Consider their background, level of expertise, and specific needs and pain points. This will help you tailor the course content and approach to meet their expectations and provide maximum value.

2. Choose a specific topic or niche: Select a topic or niche for your course that aligns with your expertise and is in high demand. Focus on a specific area where you can provide unique insights and solutions.

3. Develop course objectives: Clearly define the objectives of your course. What do you want learners to achieve by the end of the course? Set measurable goals that learners can work towards throughout the course.

4. Create a course outline: Break down the course content into modules or lessons. Each module/lesson should cover a specific topic or concept. Outline the key points, learning objectives, and activities for each module/lesson.

5. Craft engaging content: Develop high-quality content for each module/lesson. Include a mix of text, images, videos, quizzes, and practical exercises to keep learners engaged. Use storytelling techniques, real-life examples, and case studies to make the content relatable and memorable.

6. Add interactive elements: Incorporate interactive elements into your course to enhance the learning experience. This can include discussion forums, live Q&A sessions, group projects, and feedback mechanisms. Encourage learners to interact with each other and with you as the course instructor.

7. Create assessments and quizzes: Design assessments and quizzes to test learners' understanding and progress. This will help them evaluate their own learning and reinforce key concepts.

8. Provide continuous support: Offer ongoing support to learners throughout the course. This can include regular check-ins, answering questions, providing additional resources, and hosting virtual office hours. Make yourself available to address any concerns or difficulties learners may face.

9. Set a fair price: Determine a fair and competitive price for your course. Research similar courses in the market and consider factors such as the course length, value provided, and your expertise. Remember to factor in any costs or expenses associated with creating and hosting the course.

10. Develop a marketing strategy: Once your course is ready, develop a marketing strategy to promote and sell it. Identify the best channels to reach your target audience, such as social media, email marketing, webinars, or partnerships with influencers. Create compelling sales copy and use persuasive techniques to convince potential learners of the value of your course.

11. Analyze and optimize: Continuously monitor the performance of your course and collect feedback from learners. Use this data to make improvements and updates to the content, structure, or delivery methods. Stay updated with industry trends and incorporate new techniques or technologies to enhance the learning experience.

Idea 35: Custom Story Commissions

Transform your passion into a profitable endeavor by offering personalized story writing services. Perhaps help a wedding Officiator, with a story to include in his services, with this prompt:

As an imaginative storyteller, your task is to create a custom and personalized short story that will captivate the hearts of the wedding couple and their guests. Your story should reflect the unique journey of the couple and celebrate their love and commitment. Incorporate key moments and memories from their relationship, weaving them into a heartwarming narrative that resonates with the emotions of the audience. Pay attention to the details and emotions, using descriptive language and vibrant imagery to bring the story to life.

Consider the following details when crafting your story:

[Information on how the couple first met]

[Significant milestones in their relationship, such as romantic getaways, shared adventures, or overcoming challenges together]

[Special memories they have created, such as inside jokes, favorite places, or meaningful traditions]

[Input the preferred tone, i.e. serious or funny]

Your story should be engaging, heartwarming, and leave a lasting impression on the couple and their loved ones.

Idea 36: Technical Documentation

Offer to create valuable technical documentation for companies, by exploring this prompt:

As a skilled technical writer, your task is to create comprehensive technical documentation for a business. This documentation should provide detailed information about the business's products or services, including installation guides, usage instructions, troubleshooting tips, and other relevant technical information. You should ensure that the documentation is clear, concise, and easy to understand for both technical and non-technical users. Pay attention to organizing the information in a logical and intuitive manner, using headings, subheadings, and bullet points to improve readability.

To get started, please provide the following information:

[Input the name of the business]

[Input a brief description of the products or services offered]

[Input any specific features or technical aspects that should be highlighted in the documentation]

Once you have gathered the necessary information, you can begin writing the technical documentation. Remember to include step-by-step instructions, diagrams, screenshots, and any other visual aids that can help users understand the information better. It is important to consider the target audience's technical knowledge and ensure that the documentation is accessible to both beginners and experts.

Throughout the documentation, focus on clarity, accuracy, and completeness. Anticipate potential user questions or issues and address them in the documentation. Additionally, consider providing links or references to additional resources, such as tutorials or FAQs, to further support the users.

Remember to proofread and edit your work to ensure there are no errors, and consider seeking feedback from users to further improve the documentation

**Bonus Tip: Find a plug-in that can read a URL or a PDF (such as LinkReader or MixerBox), and have it first analyze the company's website information! Try this prompt:

*Use link reader plugin: Analyze the following website. Do not provide any feedback, just analyze for now and wait further instruction: [**Input link to company or product information**]*

Idea 37: Newsletter Services

Reach out to local businesses, to see if they'd be interested in a newsletter service for their customers and whip up an easy newsletter, with the help of prompt:

As a professional newsletter writer, your task is to create a compelling and engaging newsletter for the user's business. The newsletter should effectively communicate the latest updates, promotions, and news related to the business in a way that resonates with the target audience. Your goal is to captivate the readers' attention, provide valuable information, and inspire action.

To begin, gather all the relevant information about the business, including recent achievements, upcoming events, new products or services, and any special offers or discounts. Use this information to craft a catchy headline that grabs the readers' attention and entices them to keep reading.

In the body of the newsletter, highlight the key points and benefits of the updates or promotions. Use persuasive language to emphasize the value that the business brings to its customers and explain how these updates will enhance their lives or meet their needs. Incorporate engaging visuals, such as high-quality images or videos, to make the newsletter visually appealing.

Include a clear call-to-action that prompts the readers to take the desired action, whether it's visiting the website, making a purchase, attending an event, or signing up for a newsletter subscription. Make the call-to-action prominent and easily clickable or actionable.

Finally, personalize the newsletter by addressing the readers directly and establishing a friendly and approachable tone. Use storytelling techniques to create a connection with the readers and make the content more relatable and engaging.

[Input the specific details about your business or community, including any recent news, updates, promotions, or events. Include any unique aspects of your

business and its offerings. Include details about your target audience]

Example: Our business recently launched a new line of eco-friendly products. We have an upcoming sale event next week with discounts up to 30%. We also want to highlight our commitment to sustainability and how our products contribute to a greener planet. The newsletter should invite customers to visit our website and explore the new product range

---

Idea 38: Legal Document Drafts

Have a knack for the legal side of things? Draft contracts, motions or briefs, with this prompt:

As a skilled contract drafter, your role is to create a comprehensive and legally binding contract that ensures the rights and obligations of all parties involved. To accomplish this, you will need to consider the specific terms and conditions that need to be included in the contract, such as the scope of work, payment terms, dispute resolution procedures, confidentiality clauses, termination clauses, and any other relevant provisions.

To draft the contract, you should start by clearly identifying the parties involved, including their legal names and addresses. Next, outline the purpose of the contract and provide a detailed description of the goods or services to be provided. Specify any deliverables, deadlines, or milestones that need to be met.

Include provisions regarding payment, such as the amount, method, and timing of payment. Determine whether any late fees or interest charges will apply for overdue payments.

Address any intellectual property considerations, including ownership and licensing rights for any developed works or inventions.

Consider including clauses that govern dispute resolution, such as arbitration or mediation processes, to provide a fair and efficient mechanism for resolving conflicts.

Include confidentiality clauses to protect sensitive information that may be shared during the course of the contract.

Finally, clearly outline the termination provisions, specifying the conditions under which either party can terminate the agreement and any associated penalties or obligations.

[Gather all necessary details relevant to the contract, including party information, scope of work, payment terms, and any specific clauses or conditions that need to be addressed. Use these details to fill in the sections of the contract as outlined in the prompt.]

Example: Parties: XYZ Corporation and John Smith. Scope of Work: Development of a custom software application. Payment Terms: $50,000 upon completion, with a late fee of 2% per month for overdue payments. Intellectual Property: XYZ Corporation retains all rights to the software. Dispute Resolution: Any disputes will be resolved through arbitration. Confidentiality: Both parties agree to keep project details confidential. Termination: Either party may terminate with 30 days' notice

Idea 39: Resume Writing Services

Offer resume writing services to those in need, on gig economy apps like UpWork or TaskRabbit. Try this prompt:

*Act as a professional resume writer and create a polished and impactful resume that highlights the candidate's skills, qualifications, and accomplishments. Use a clean and organized format, with clear headings and bullet points to make it easy to read and navigate. Tailor the resume to the specific job or industry the candidate is applying for [**Input details of the job listing, if available**], and include relevant keywords to ensure it passes through applicant tracking systems. Use concise and action-oriented language to describe the candidate's experience and achievements, focusing on results and measurable outcomes. Proofread carefully for grammar and spelling errors, and ensure that the resume is tailored to the specific job requirements and showcases the candidate's unique value proposition.*

Begin by including the candidate's full name, contact information (phone number, email address), and a professional summary or objective statement at the top of the resume.

Create sections for the candidate's education, work experience, skills, and any relevant certifications or additional qualifications.

For each section, organize the information in reverse chronological order (most recent first).

When describing work experience, include the dates of employment, job titles, company names, and concise bullet points highlighting key responsibilities and achievements.

Emphasize any quantifiable results or outcomes achieved in each role, such as increased sales, cost savings, or successful project completions.

Include a section for relevant skills, both hard and soft skills, that align with the job requirements.

If applicable, mention any honors, awards, or publications that showcase the candidate's expertise.

Tailor the resume to the specific job or industry by incorporating keywords from the job description.

Keep the resume concise and to the point, preferably fitting on one page (unless the candidate has extensive experience).

Candidate: **Gather and input all necessary information about the candidate, including their work history, education, skills, and any other relevant details***.*

Example: Candidate: John Doe, Contact: [email address], 555-1234. Professional Summary: Experienced project manager with over 10 years in the IT industry. Education: MBA from XYZ University. Work Experience: Project Manager at ABC Corp (2015-2021), Key Achievements: Led a team of 20, successfully delivered 15+ major projects, Skills: Leadership, Agile Methodologies, Communication, Time Management

Idea 40: Voice-Over Scripts

Find YouTube videos in need of voice-over scripts, and offer to sell them to the creator. Give this prompt a try:

As an expert scriptwriter, your task is to create a captivating and engaging voice-over script for a YouTube video about **[Input the main topic of theme of video. Identify key points, the tone, and the style of the voice-over. Input your target audience and the video's goal.** *Example: Our video focuses on the benefits of sustainable living. The key points include reducing carbon footprint, saving costs, and promoting a healthier lifestyle. The tone should be informative yet engaging, aimed at young adults interested in environmental conservation].*

The script should grab the viewer's attention from the beginning and keep them hooked throughout. Utilize a conversational and friendly tone to connect with the audience and make the information easily digestible. Incorporate storytelling elements, relevant examples, and anecdotes to make the script relatable and memorable.

Consider the following structure for the script:

Attention-grabbing introduction: Start with a compelling hook that immediately captures the viewer's interest and introduces the topic of the video.

Problem identification: Clearly outline the problem or pain point that the video will address. Highlight the significance of the issue and how it affects the viewer.

Solution presentation: Introduce the solution or the main theme of the video. Present the benefits and advantages of using the product, service, or concept being discussed.

Explanation with visuals: Break down the information into easily understandable segments. Use visuals, graphics, or demonstrations where appropriate to enhance the viewer's understanding.

Call-to-action: Encourage the viewer to take action, whether it's subscribing to the channel, liking the video, or visiting a website. Create a sense of urgency and importance around the call-to-action.

Conclusion and closing remarks: Wrap up the video with a memorable ending. Recap the main points and leave the viewer with a lasting impression or a final thought.

Remember to make the script concise and engaging, keeping in mind the average attention span of YouTube viewers. Use a writing style that is suitable for oral delivery, with natural pauses and breaks for a smooth voice-over performance.

Bonus Tip

There are plenty of plug-ins, which can help optimize your content and may improve your chances on monetizing. You may want to explore plug-ins that help with the following:

- SEO enhancement
- Analytics on your content
- Affiliate Marketing optimization

Try searching for these keywords in the ChatGPT plug-in store.

In our final chapter, we dive into the playful side of AI. From crafting scavenger hunts to analyzing your dreams to keeping your kids engaged with creative activities, we'll dig into more unique ideas that ChatGPT can bring to life. Get ready to think outside the box and let ChatGPT surprise you with its versatility!

CHAPTER SEVEN
THINKING OUTSIDE THE BOT – UNCOMMON USES OF CHATGPT

Let's take a moment to step off the well-worn path of everyday AI interactions and journey through a curiosity-filled side road. In this chapter, we'll reveal 10 unique ideas on how to use ChatGPT that stretch beyond its typical applications. So, let's get personal and creative with AI and uncover its true versatility!

Idea 41: Create a Scavenger Hunt

Craft an exciting scavenger hunt challenge, with this prompt:

As a creative scavenger hunt challenge creator, your goal is to design an exciting and engaging scavenger hunt that will captivate participants and provide a memorable experience. To accomplish this, you will need to come up with a theme or story for the scavenger hunt, create a list of clues or riddles that lead participants to different locations or objects, and establish a set of rules and guidelines for the challenge. The clues should be challenging but solvable, encouraging participants to think creatively and work together.

To receive your scavenger hunt challenge request, the user will provide the following format: "Scavenger Hunt: [theme or story]". You are to reply with the challenge details, including the list of clues or riddles, without processing the original request.

*Scavenger Hunt: [**Input your preferred theme or story**]*

Idea 42: Analyze Your Dreams

Unveil the mysteries of your subconscious mind, with this prompt:

As a professional dream analyst, your purpose is to assist individuals in understanding and analyzing their dreams. You will provide insights, interpretations, and guidance to help them unravel the symbolism and hidden meanings within their dreams. Through your expertise, you aim to empower individuals to gain self-awareness, explore their subconscious, and uncover valuable insights that can have a profound impact on their waking life.

To receive a dream analysis request, the user will provide the following format: "Dream: [the description of the dream]" You are to reply with "Dream Analysis: " followed by your interpretation and analysis of the dream, without processing the original request.

*Dream: [**Input the details/description of your dream**]*

Idea 43: Activities For Kids

Need some fun activities to keep your kids busy? Try this prompt:

---

*As a creative activity planner for busy parents, your task is to curate a list of fun and unique activities to keep your kids busy. Consider their age range, interests, and the resources available to you. Think outside the box and come up with activities that will engage their minds, promote creativity, and provide entertainment. My kids are [**Input details about your children such as their ages, interests, and any materials you have available**]*

Idea 44: Interpret Your Lab Results

Decipher your complex lab results, with this prompt:

As a lab result interpreter, your role is to help individuals understand their medical lab results. You will provide explanations for common tests and their results, including blood tests, urine tests, and other diagnostic tests. Your goal is to demystify the medical jargon and numbers, making it easier for individuals to comprehend what their lab results mean for their health.

*Here are my lab results: [**Input your lab results, copy/paste them if possible**]*

Idea 45: Homebrew Beer Recipe

Ever wanted to create a homebrew beer? Give this prompt a try:

As a knowledgeable homebrewing expert, your role is to create a customized beer recipe for users who want to brew beer at home. To achieve this, you should consider the user's preferences in terms of beer style, flavor profile, and desired alcohol content. Additionally, take into account the availability of ingredients and equipment for homebrewing.

To receive your personalized recipe, the user will provide the following details in the specified format: Beer Style: **[preferred beer style]**

Flavor Profile: **[desired flavors, e.g., hoppy, malty, fruity]**

Alcohol Content: **[desired ABV]**

Ingredients Available: **[list of available ingredients]**

Idea 46: DIY Project Guides

Create a project guide for your next DIY adventure. Give this prompt a try:

As a skilled DIY project guide creator, your task is to create a detailed and comprehensive guide for a specific do-it-yourself project. Your guide should provide step-by-step instructions, along with any necessary materials, tools, and safety precautions. It should be written in a clear and concise manner, ensuring that even beginners can follow along easily. Include any additional tips, tricks, or alternative methods that may help enhance the project.

To receive your task, the user will provide the following format: "Project: [project name]"

You are to reply with 'Project Guide: ' followed by your detailed project guide, without processing the original request.

*Project: [**Input details of your project**]*

Example: Project: Build a wooden bookshelf that is 5ft tall by 3ft wide and 1ft deep

---

Idea 47: Fantasy Sports Analysis

Elevate your fantasy sports game with AI-powered analytics. Give this prompt a try:

As an expert fantasy sports analyst, I will provide you with a thorough analysis of your fantasy sports team, enabling you to gain a competitive edge over your rivals. I will evaluate your team's current composition, strengths, weaknesses, and potential areas for improvement. By considering player performance, upcoming fixtures, and team dynamics, I will develop a strategic plan tailored to maximize your team's performance.

To proceed, please provide the following details:

List of players in your fantasy sports team

Desired sport (e.g., football, basketball, baseball, etc.)

League rules and scoring system

Once I have this information, I will analyze your team and formulate a comprehensive strategy that includes:

Player Analysis: Evaluating the performance, consistency, and potential of each player in your team. Identifying top performers, potential sleepers, and players underperforming.

Matchup Analysis: Analyzing upcoming fixtures, opponent strength, and any favorable opportunities to exploit.

Team Composition: Assessing the balance of your team across different positions and identifying areas where you may need additional strength or depth.

Trading and Waiver Wire Strategies: Providing advice on potential trades, waiver wire pickups, and player drops to optimize your team's talent and address any weaknesses.

Captaincy and Starting Lineup Strategies: Advising on selecting the right players for captaincy and determining the best starting lineup based on performance, matchups, and injuries.

By implementing the insights gained through this analysis, you will be able to make well-informed decisions that will give you a competitive advantage over your opponents and increase your chances of winning in fantasy sports.

[Input your list of players, or desired players, on your fantasy sports team]

[Input the sport]

[Input your fantasy league rules or scoring system]

Example: My fantasy football team includes Tom Brady, Derrick Henry, DeAndre Hopkins, and Travis Kelce. We play in a PPR league with standard scoring rules

---

Idea 48: Custom Workout Challenges

Personalize your workout challenges, with this prompt:

Act as a fitness coach and create a personalized workout challenge for an individual looking to improve their fitness and reach their goals. Consider the individual's fitness level, preferences, and any specific areas they want to target. Design a structured workout plan that includes a combination of cardiovascular exercises, strength training, and flexibility exercises. Set achievable goals and milestones to keep them motivated throughout the challenge. Provide detailed instructions for each exercise, including the number of repetitions or duration, proper form and technique, and any modifications or progressions. Encourage the individual to track their progress and make adjustments as needed. Remember to provide support and motivation throughout the challenge to help them stay committed and achieve their desired results

[Input specific details about the individual's fitness level, goals, preferences, and any special considerations (like injuries or medical conditions)]

Example: I'm creating a workout plan for a 30-year-old woman with moderate fitness level. She aims to improve her overall strength and flexibility, with a focus on core and lower body. She prefers a mix of cardio and strength training and has no known injuries

---

Idea 49: Recipe Remix

Find a recipe remix with those leftover ingredients, with this prompt:

As a creative recipe developer, your task is to create a delicious and inventive food dish using leftover ingredients. Your goal is to come up with a recipe that is easy to follow, utilizes the available ingredients, and results in a tasty and satisfying meal. Consider the flavors and textures of the ingredients and experiment with different cooking techniques to bring out their best qualities.

[Input the specific leftover ingredients you have available and any dietary preferences or restrictions.]

Example: I have leftover grilled chicken, bell peppers, and rice. I prefer dishes with a bit of spice and enjoy Asian flavors

To create your recipe, follow these steps:

Take inventory of the leftover ingredients and assess their freshness and quality. Discard any items that are spoiled or past their prime.

Identify the main component of the dish based on the largest quantity of leftover ingredients. For example, if you have leftover chicken and vegetables, you may choose to create a stir-fry.

Determine the supporting ingredients that will complement the main component. These could include pantry staples like garlic, onions, herbs, spices, or sauces.

Prepare the ingredients by cleaning, chopping, or slicing them as necessary.

Heat a pan or skillet over medium heat and add oil or butter. Sauté the onions and garlic until fragrant.

Add the main component, such as the leftover chicken, and cook until heated through.

Add the supporting ingredients, such as the vegetables, and stir-fry until they are tender-crisp.

Season the dish with herbs, spices, or sauces to enhance the flavors. Taste and adjust the seasonings as needed.

Serve the dish hot and garnish with fresh herbs or a sprinkle of cheese, if desired.

Idea 50: Personalized Joke Writer

Need some new dad (or mom) jokes? Give this prompt a try:

As a humorous parent-friendly joke generator, your task is to provide a collection of funny and age-appropriate jokes that parents can tell their kids. These jokes should be light-hearted and entertaining, while also promoting positive family interactions and creating moments of laughter. Keep in mind the age range of the children and ensure that the jokes are suitable for their understanding and sense of humor. Emphasize clean humor that can be enjoyed by the whole family.

To receive your request, the user will provide the following format: 'Jokes for parents to tell their kids.'

[Input details on the age range of your kids and any specific humor preferences they have.]

Example: Looking for jokes suitable for kids aged 6-10, preferably with a focus on animal and food-related humor

Here are a few examples to get you started:

Why don't scientists trust atoms? Because they make up everything!

How does a penguin build its house? Igloos it together!

What do you call cheese that isn't yours? Nacho cheese!

Why did the teddy bear say 'no' to dessert? Because it was already stuffed!

What did one wall say to the other wall? I'll meet you at the corner!

Why don't skeletons fight each other? They don't have the guts!

I hope you feel inspired by the less-traveled paths we've explored together. These 10 unique ideas were designed to stretch your imagination and showcase the true versatility of ChatGPT. Remember, the journey with AI is as much about creativity and personal expression as it is about technology. As we move towards the conclusion of this book, let's carry forward this spirit of exploration and innovation, ready to apply the endless possibilities of ChatGPT in our lives. The world of AI is vast and ever-evolving, and you're now equipped to be a part of that exciting journey.

CONCLUSION

As we close the final pages of "ChatGPT for Newbies," I hope you feel a sense of accomplishment and excitement. You've journeyed through artificial intelligence, transforming from a beginner to someone who can confidently navigate and utilize ChatGPT in various aspects of your life. This book was not just about understanding AI; it was about making it a valuable part of your daily routine, whether for productivity, creativity, content creation, or even monetizing your skills.

Reflect on your journey from the first chapter, where ChatGPT was a new concept, to now, where you have 50 practical and innovative ideas at your fingertips. You've unlocked the potential of ChatGPT through prompts, enhanced your work and productivity, explored the realms of creativity and arts, boosted your content creation and social media presence, discovered ways to monetize these skills, and even delved into uncommon and fun uses of this versatile tool.

Remember, the world of AI and technology is ever-evolving, and so is your journey. The end of this book is just the beginning of your adventure with ChatGPT. As you continue to learn and experiment, you'll find even more ways to integrate this powerful tool into your life.

I am excited about the future and the possibility of sharing more insights and advancements with you. The landscape of AI is vast and full of potential, and I am already pondering new ideas and applications for future books. So, keep an eye out! With the power of AI, there's always more to learn, more to discover, and more to create.

Thank you for choosing to embark on this journey with "ChatGPT for Newbies." Your curiosity and willingness to learn and adapt are what make the exploration of technology so rewarding. I can't wait to see where your newfound knowledge and skills take you. Here's to a future where AI is not just a tool but a companion in your journey of growth and innovation.

Until we meet again in the pages of the next book, keep exploring, keep learning, and most importantly, keep enjoying the journey into the fascinating world of AI!

Made in the USA
Las Vegas, NV
10 December 2023

82407828R00066